# "POLOVTSIAN DANCES"
## AND
# "IN THE STEPPES OF CENTRAL ASIA"
## IN FULL SCORE

## ALEXANDER BORODIN

DOVER PUBLICATIONS, INC.
MINEOLA, NEW YORK

*Bibliographical Note*

This Dover edition, first published in 1997, is a new compilation of two works original-
ly published separately; spelling variants of their titles are given as published: *Alexander
Borodin / Polovetsian Dances from the opera "Prince Igor"* was originally published in an
authoritative edition, n.d.; *Alexander Porphyriewitsch Borodin / Eine Steppenskizze aus Mittel-
Asien* was originally published as Edition Eulenberg No. 833 by Ernst Eulenburg Ltd.,
London, n.d.

The Dover edition adds an integrated, expanded table of contents, program notes, lists
of instrumentation, and new headings for the sections of "Polovtsian Dances." The infor-
mation about the composition of *In the Steppes of Central Asia* originally appeared on the
title page of the Eulenberg edition; that work's program note is freely translated from the
French "Programme" in the same edition.

*International Standard Book Number: 0-486-29556-7*

Manufactured in the United States of America
Dover Publications, Inc., 31 East 2nd Street, Mineola, N.Y. 11501

# Contents

Composed 1880 for a representation of *tableaux
vivants* on the occasion of the 25th anniversary
of the accession of Tsar Alexander II

Borodin worked on his opera *Prince Igor* in the years 1869–70 and 1874–87, but the music remained unfinished at his death, 27 February 1887. The score was revised, completed and partly orchestrated by Nikolay Rimsky-Korsakov and Alexander Glazunov. The present concert version of the "Polovtsian Dances," extracted from Act II of the opera and orchestrated by Rimsky-Korsakov, was premiered in St. Petersburg, 11 March 1879. The full opera was first performed in the same city on 4 November 1890.

# POLOVTSIAN DANCES
## Instrumentation

Piccolo  [Flauto piccolo., Fl. picc.]
2 Flutes  [Flauti, Fl.]
2 Oboes  [Oboe, Ob.]
English Horn  [Corno inglese, C.ingl.]
2 Clarinets in A, B♭ ("B") [Clarinetti, Cl.]
2 Bassoons  [Fagotti, Fg.]

4 Horns in F  [Corni, Cor.]
2 Trumpets in A, B♭ ("B") [Trombe, Tr.]
3 Trombones  [Tromboni, Trb.]
Tuba  [Tuba]

Timpani  [Timpani, Timp.]

Percussion:
   Bell (Glockenspiel) [Campanella, Camp.]
   Triangle  [Triangolo, Trgl.]
   Tambourine  [Tamburino. T'runo]
   Snare Drum  [Tamburo, Tamb.]
   Cymbals  [Piatti]
   Bass Drum  [Cassa]

Harp  [Arpa, Arp.]

Violins I, II  [Violini, Vl.]
Violas  [Viole, Vle.]
Cellos  [Violoncelli, Vcl.]
Basses  [Contrabassi, Cb.]

# Polovtsian Dances

From the opera *Prince Igor*

## Introduction

# First Dance

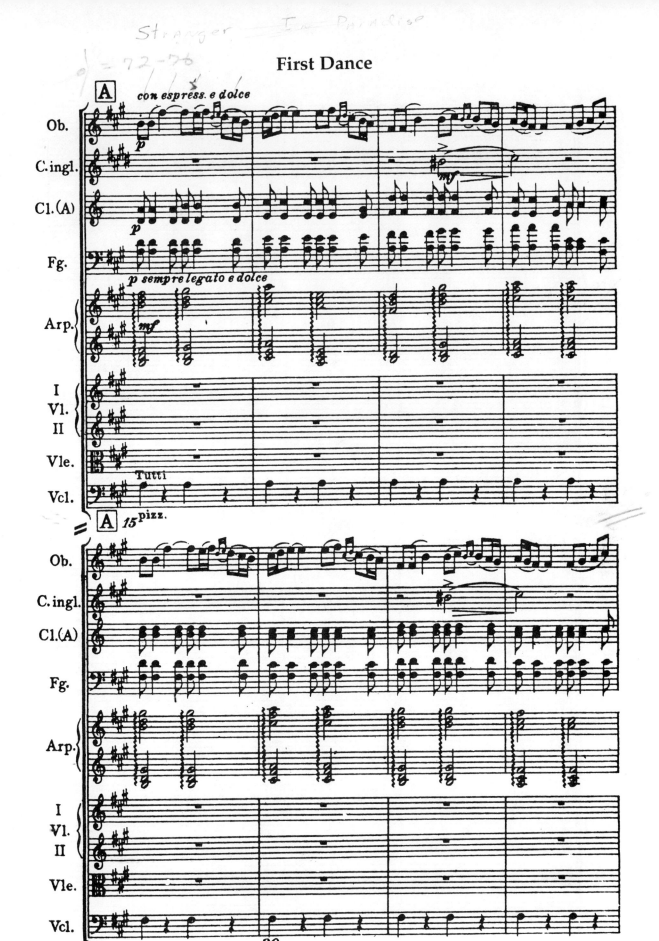

6    *Polovtsian Dances* (1)

## Second Dance

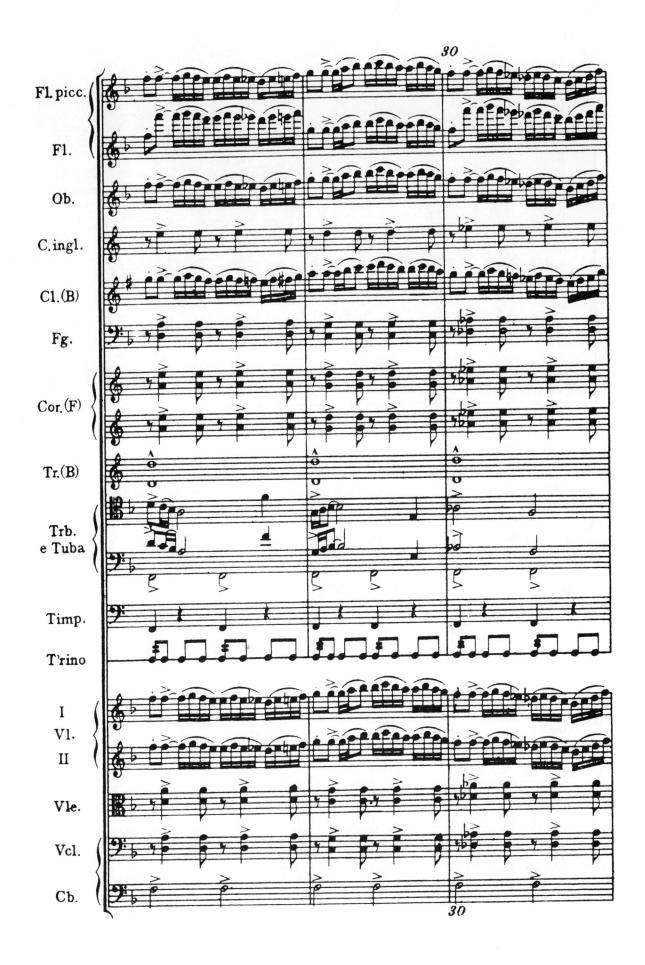

# Third Dance

# Fourth Dance

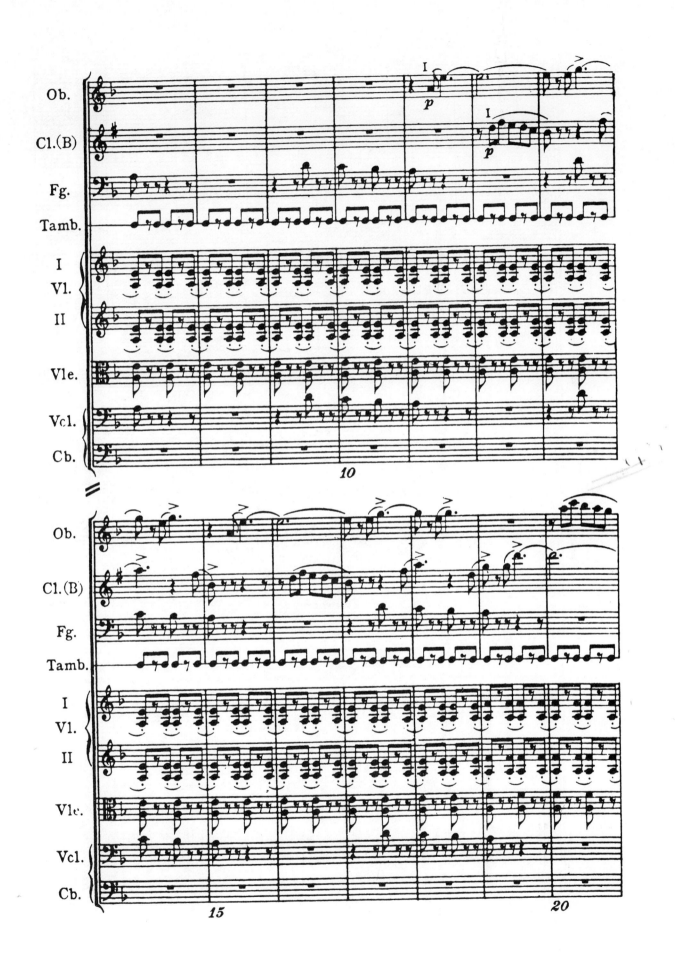

*Polovtsian Dances* (4)

# First Dance
*(reprise)*

*Polovtsian Dances* (1, *reprise*)

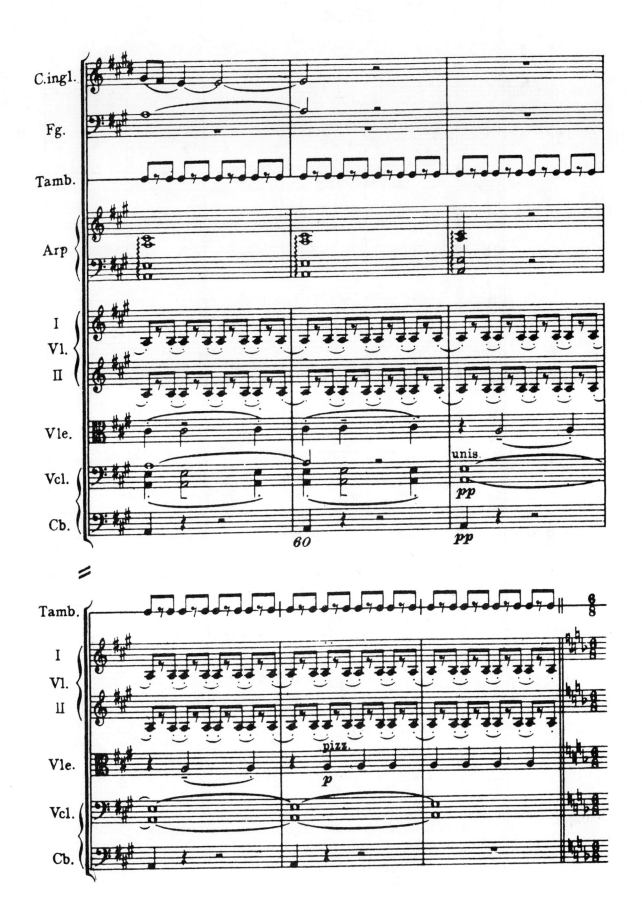

# Fourth Dance
*(reprise)*

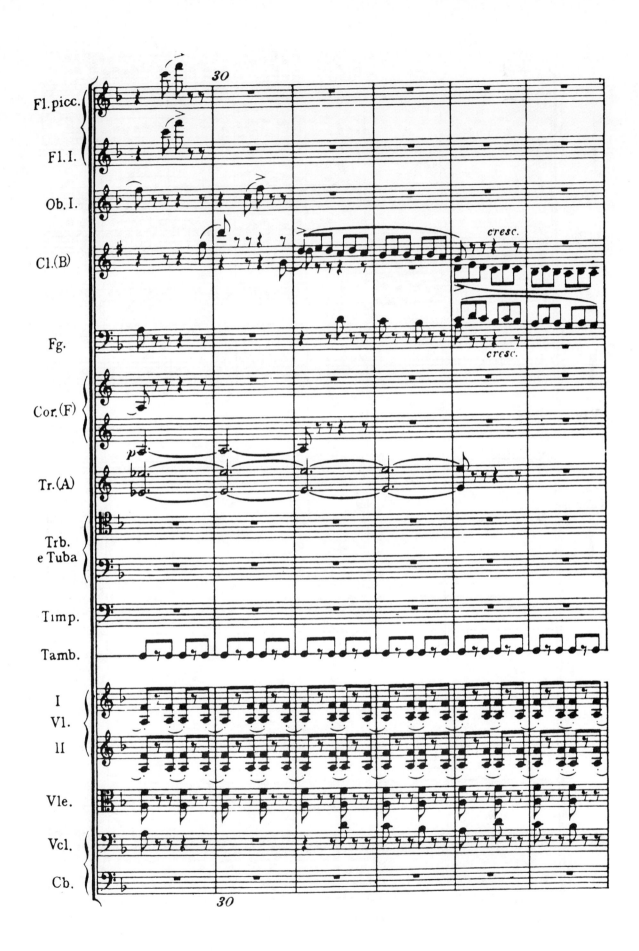

*Polovtsian Dances* (4, *reprise*)

# Second Dance
*(reprise)*

*Polovtsian Dances* (2, *reprise*)

# Coda

*Polovtsian Dances* (Coda)

"In the silence of the sandy steppes of Central Asia unfolds the refrain of a peaceful Russian song, never before heard there. We hear as well the melancholy sounds of Eastern song, and the hoofbeats of approaching horses and camels. Escorted in safety by Russian soldiers, a caravan crosses the vast desert, confidently continuing its long, relentless journey. Russian songs and Asiatic melodies blend in a common harmony, their refrains heard far into the desert, finally fading away in the great distance."

—Freely translated from the French "Programme" in the original edition

# IN THE STEPPES OF CENTRAL ASIA
## Instrumentation

2 Flutes [Flauti, Fl.]
2 Oboes [Oboe, Ob.]
English Horn [Corno inglese, C.ingl.]
2 Clarinets in A [Clarinetti, Clar.]
2 Bassoons [Fagotti, Fag.]

4 Horns in F [Corni, Cor.]
2 Trumpets in F [Trombe, Tbe.]
3 Trombone  [Tromboni, Tbni.]

Timpani [Timpani, Timp.]

Violins I, II [Violino, Vl.]
Violas [Viola, Vla.]
Cellos [Violoncello, Vc.]
Basses [Contrabasso, Cb.]

*Most respectfully dedicated to Dr. Franz Liszt*

# In the Steppes of Central Asia

101

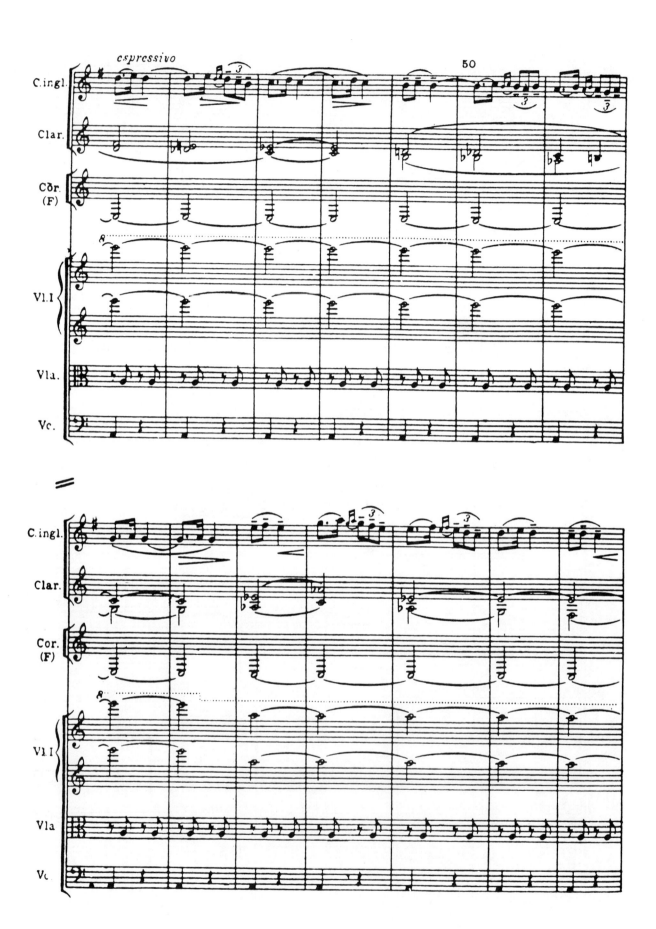

*In the Steppes of Central Asia*

*In the Steppes of Central Asia*

*In the Steppes of Central Asia*

END OF EDITION